CW01494800

Jobs in Sport

Written by
Cath Jones

Ransⓘm

There are lots of jobs you can do when you are an adult.

You might be a gardener, or a vet ... or a drummer.

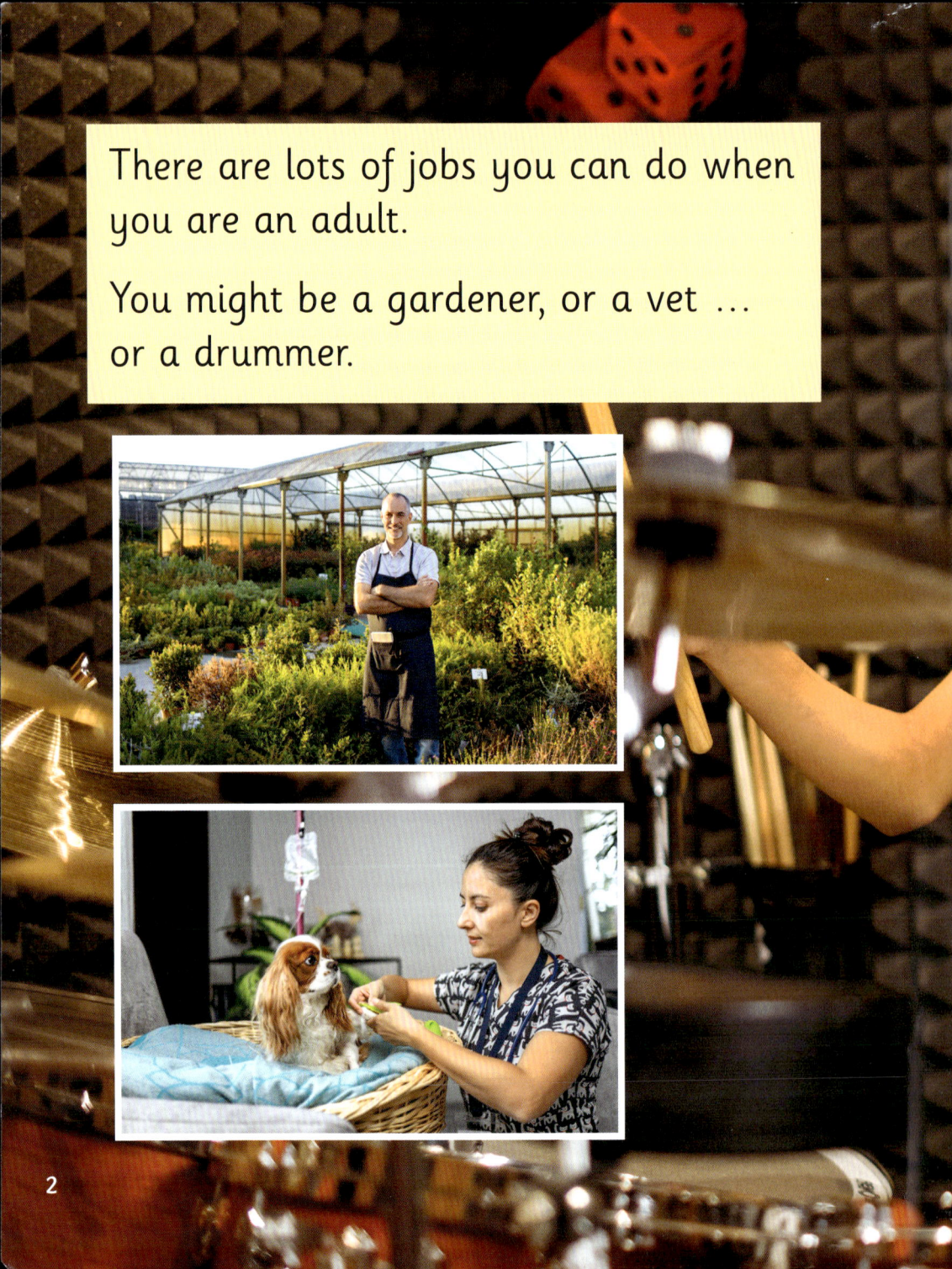

But what if you are good at sport?

What jobs can you do in sport?

Can swimming be a job? Yes, it can!

This swimmer swims for fun, but the best swimmers can do it as a job.

They need to train hard, but the best swimmers can win medals.

If you have a job in sport, you need to be the best. You need to keep fit.

This man is a fitness trainer. So is she. They will help you keep fit.

This trainer is helping this man get fit. He runs and bends and lifts bar bells.

She checks how fit he is. Is he getting stronger?

Running helps you keep fit.
Can running be a job too?

Yes, it can!

This runner runs for her job.
She might win some medals.

Jumping can be a job too.

Some jumpers do it for fun.
But the best jumpers do it for a job.

For this sort of jumping, you must have
no fear!

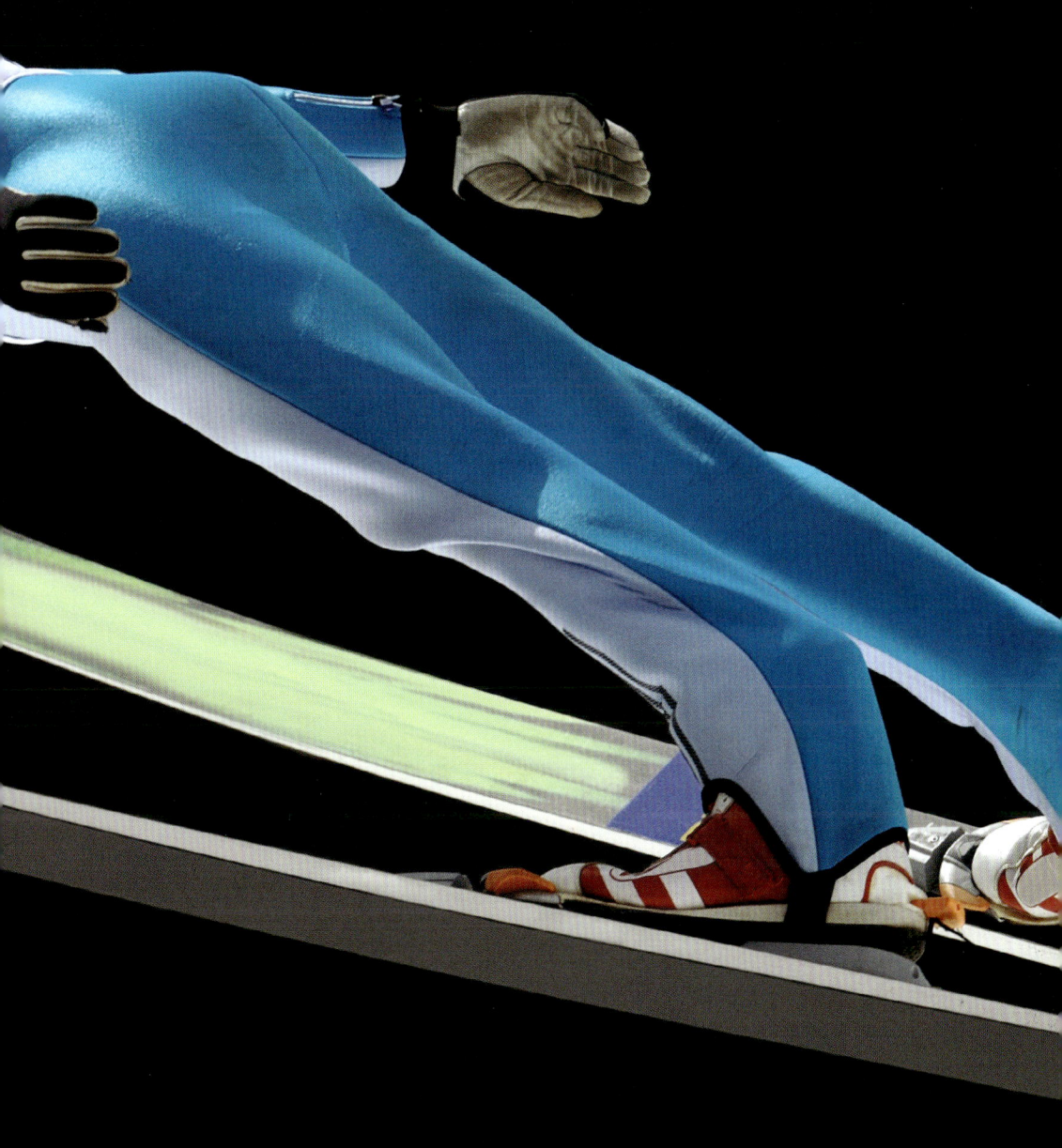

This sport is the high jump.

How high can she jump? Can she win a medal?

This is the long jump.

How far do you think she can jump?

You can get jobs in all sorts of sports.

You might have a job in athletics, tennis, sailing or surfing.

You might be a cook. In sports, they must have the best food.

Or will you look after all the kit?

A job in sport can be a thrill, but it is hard. You must keep on getting better and better!